Cracking the $$ Code:
WHAT SUCCESSFUL MEN KNOW AND YOU DON'T (YET)

To the memory of the late Barbara Connolly Hughes,
an inspirational mentor

Table of Contents

Introduction...9

CODE NUMBER ONE: Know Your Own Worth...............................13

CODE NUMBER TWO: Set Goals.....................................23

CODE NUMBER THREE: Get a Contract..29

CODE NUMBER FOUR: Partnering is Key........................35

CODE NUMBER FIVE: Image is Important......................................47

CODE NUMBER SIX: Take Risks.....................................55

CODE NUMBER SEVEN: Persistence Wins the Race......................63

Conclusion 75

Recommended Resources...77

Acknowledgements 80

Introduction

WOMEN SPEND A SIGNIFICANT AMOUNT OF TIME FOCUSING ON THE NEEDS and wants of everyone else in their lives. This is a key strength, but it is also a key weakness. If you don't make a conscious, disciplined effort to shift that focus back to yourself and think about the importance of protecting yourself when you are connecting with others, there is a great risk that you will undercut yourself.

All women need to remember what the flight attendant says at the beginning of each flight: "If you are traveling with a small child and the oxygen mask drops, put that mask over your own face first. It is only when you are strong enough to take care of yourself that you will have the strength to take care of that child."

Those instructions are valid for women in more situations than a crisis in the air. They apply to a woman's role at home, at work and in the community.

Psychoanalyst Jean Baker Miller, the author of *Toward a New Psychology of Women*, and first director of the Stone Center at Wellesley College, developed the "Relational-Cultural Theory" with her colleagues. Their work suggests that all growth occurs in connection, that all people yearn for connection, and that growth-fostering relationships are created through mutual empathy and empowerment.

The other side of this is *disconnection* – when the relationship connections no longer work or have become uncomfortable. When this happens, if the less powerful person is able to express her feelings and the other person is able to respond empathetically, disconnection can actually lead to a strengthened relationship and a strengthened sense of relational competence. If, however, the injured or less powerful person is unable to express her feelings or receives a response of indifference, she will begin to keep aspects of herself out of the relationship in order to maintain the relationship.

This very complicated analysis is at the heart of the difference between men and women in the work force. Because so much of what a woman values is the connection and the relationship with others, when that is not reciprocated or encouraged, it impedes a woman's ability to succeed.

Men, on the other hand, don't have that problem. They measure their success on their individual ability to get ahead and are not as bogged down by how they are judged in relationships with others.

They are also not afraid of ruffling the feathers of those they work with to achieve success. The fear of controversy impedes women from attaining higher levels of success because women do not instinctively understand that ruffling feathers and creating controversy does not mean that the relation-ship will end; in fact, it can mean that working through that will improve the relationship and lead to greater success for all.

Women are afraid to risk the relationship for personal reward. This fundamental difference in the way that men and women approach success in the business world has led me to investigate what the practical underpin-nings of this difference are – what is it that men know that allows them to individuate success and that women don't know because they are so focused on the relationship with others.

In this book I have set forth important codes that successful men have already deciphered and women just don't know exist, but can easily uncover. They are invisible lessons, secret lessons, lessons that men do not intuit and can not sit down by themselves and figure out intellectually. They are les-sons that are hard wired into successful men's brains, not women's brains. The codes strung together in this book, when used in tandem, teach women how to crack the $$ code that men already know.

None of them were obvious until I learned them. Once I learned them, I did not understand how I could not have known them before.

As an attorney I started off like all other associates, working long hours, six days a week and aspiring (some day) to become partner. There was no road map, no rule book, just watching and observing what everyone else did and wanting to stay in step. I went down roads and hit brick walls, then stood up and tried to figure out how to do it better. It took me a long time to realize that success required more than brains and hard work, and that men seemed to have an inside track. Why?

Figuring that out took time, but it was time well spent.

I went from associate to partner, then had my own law firm for ten years, then joined another law firm and now head a department there. As an attorney I have advised thousands of clients, written two technical texts and two popular books, started my own seminar business and present, on average, 36 seminars a year. I have received many awards, including being named by my peers as one of The Best Lawyers in America, a Top 50 Super-Lawyer, and Massachusetts Estate Planner of the Year.

My quest for success and my observation of the quest for success of others has taught me many lessons and allowed me to uncover the secrets that men know and women don't know. Cracking the $$ Code will help you, no matter what stage your career is in - whether you are in the workforce now or re-entering it - and no matter what your business is, because the heart of these lessons is making sure that you have put that oxygen mask squarely on yourself first, so that you remain strong and empowered to accomplish great things in the world – and in so doing protect yourself, those you love and the organizations you care about.

CODE No. 1 | Know Your Own Worth

WOMEN TEND TO SPEND MOST OF THEIR TIME STRIVING TO EXCEL, GOING for the "A" and focusing on external approval ("Atta girl, great job!") to derive a sense of accomplishment.

Going for the "A", however, is a weak and singular goal.

Men understand that they can go for the "A" and also go for making good money; and that, in fact, these are not mutually exclusive concepts. Nor are they concepts that conflict; they are collaborative concepts that go together, and when they do, you can achieve greater success. You can achieve the "A" more often and earn more money as well.

Because by nature women base their success on their relationship to others, they often make choices that are not in their best interest. Barbara Stanny, the pioneer in the field of women, money and self esteem and author of "Prince Charming Isn't Coming: How Women Get Smart About Money" and "Secrets of Six Figure Earning Women: Surprising Strategies to Up Your Earnings and Change Your Life" says the reason women don't earn what they should is not because of any external force, but rather an internal force that stems from the way they have been mapping their lives. Women give more of their time away than men do. They undervalue themselves. They give breaks to people they feel sorry for (regardless of that person's ability to pay), and they do not value themselves economically. Women will get a second job to earn more money, rather than insisting on getting what they deserve to earn in their core job.

Money is a measure of how you value your own worth and the services you provide. Women tend to undervalue themselves and their contributions. And so it is not surprising that many women tell me billing is a tricky and sometimes stressful topic. If 100% of your clients pay 100% of every bill you are sending out without any complaints, your bills are too low, and you should take a second look at the way you are charging for your services.

About ten years ago I had lunch with one of my mentors – a very accomplished woman who understood this very well and was watching me struggle with economics and relationships in the practice of law. She had a present for me wrapped up and in a box. As she handed me the box she said to me, "Whenever you do your monthly client billing, take this and put it in front of you and look at it for 60 seconds before you begin the billing process."

I opened the box and inside it was an engraved plaque shaped like a ruler, on it the words: "I WILL NO LONGER DO PRO BONO WORK FOR MULTIMILLIONAIRES."

I try very hard to be fair to myself and to my clients when I bill. On those occasions when the amount of the bill is challenged, my policy has always been to stand by the billing decision I have made, tell the client that and leave it up to them to pay what they think is fair for the services provided.

GOOD IS OFTEN GOOD ENOUGH

For many women the desire to do the best they can do puts them in the box of mastering the project. In life there is a time when "good is good enough" and it is important to move on. When I began to write a two volume, 1800 page technical book (from scratch) for a premier legal publisher, I wanted it to be the "best book" out there on the topic. It took me seven and a half years of nights and weekends to complete that project.

In hindsight, while I can understand wanting to create an extremely good product, I realize that striving for perfection was going overboard. Authoring a book that was good enough in a shorter time frame would have brought the book to market sooner, served its purpose, educated the lawyers who could have used it earlier and freed up my time to focus on other projects.

ASK FOR IT!

As Barbara Stanny writes, many women grow up believing the fairy tale that one day "Prince Charming" – a man, an inheritance, a lottery win, some other external force - will come along and financially rescue them, the damsels in distress. Believing that Prince Charming is coming on his white horse to sweep you up and rescue you handicaps you from taking the necessary personal responsibility for achieving your own financial success.

My experience is that "Prince Charming" does not have to come in the form of a huge windfall or lottery win. If you become a little more strategic, it can result from your annual compensation and salary review.

Men know that no one is going to tap them on the shoulder and say. "You have done great work. Here is a big unexpected bonus or raise." They know that they have to position themselves for that and ask for it. Women, unfortunately, are much more likely to sit there waiting for that tap on the shoulder.

When I was in high school, I wanted a summer internship or a job with The Boston Globe, and my uncle got me an interview with a man there who was very high up. The interview went well. I was sure he liked me and was therefore shocked when my uncle informed me I was going to be offered neither an unpaid internship nor the job.

Yes, he said, the man had, in fact, liked me a great deal. He had decided not to give me the job because I did not ask him for it.

I was shocked. I thought someone who liked me and saw my potential would offer me a position! It never crossed my mind to ask for it.

That does not mean I learned the "Ask for It" lesson in high school after that rejection. I had to experience being passed over because I did not ask for it a few more times before I understood what was happening.

"Don't limit yourself. Many people limit themselves to what they think they can do. You can go as far as your mind let's you. What you believe you can achieve."

— MARY KAY ASH

Asking for it is not an instinct women have. I have put a lot of thought into why that is so.

It could be fear of failure. Women worry that if they ask for it and don't get it, they have failed and not received the "A".

It could be that women take asking for it and not getting it as personal rejection. Men understand the concept of "planned rejection". This is an actual strategy to ask for something you know you won't get – yet. The rejection is planned and part of an overall strategy to put the "ask" up front and center in people's minds so that the process of asking for it will unfold and the negotiation will begin. To men, asking for it and not getting it is not personal.

It could be because women think if they ask for it, they will appear too aggressive.

It could be because women expect to be taken care of and think that someone is going to notice their good behavior and just reward them.

It could be that because women care about the relationships with their peers and feel that if they ask for it and end up ahead of the others in their peer group, they will be out of that peer group, and it's a very comfortable place to me.

Asking for it is a skill women must learn. It has taken me a very long time to learn it.

JUST SAY NO

In one of my first associate positions, I was interested in doing trusts and estates, but the real estate market was booming and the trusts and estates work was not as busy. The managing partner of the firm assigned me to work in real estate. Although I did not like real estate work, it did not occur to me that I could say no to the assignment.

Soon I was doing 12-15 condominium closings a day. The more work I did, the more work I got, but it still did not occur to me to say "no". I soldiered on and found myself driving to the lending bank's office every night at 9:00 on my way home from the office to drop off closing packages in a locked chute. I gained 10 pounds because I was always eating fast food on the fly and had to buy new clothes because I did not have time to do laundry.

That continued for six months. No one thanked me. No one gave me a raise or bonus and no one else had to work as hard. No one cared, but to be fair, why should they if I did not care enough to stick up for myself?

When I left that firm – not because of that experience but because there was not enough trusts and estates work, which is what I wanted to do - the managing partner was shocked. "You had a tremendous future here," he told me, "You are one of the best workers we have ever had!" (No kidding.)

Many women have a hard time saying "no" because of the manner in which we value relationships and the connections we create with others. We worry that if we say "no", we are letting someone down.

The reality is when we don't say "no" in certain circumstances we are demonstrating a lack of self-respect and letting ourselves down.

Hand in hand with 'Just say no' is that we all need to remember that we are our biggest asset – our minds and our time. We must remind ourselves of that, recognize it and take care of ourselves.

DELEGATE, DELEGATE, DELEGATE

If what you are doing can be just easily done by someone else who is below you in the chain of authority, then you should not doing it. That person should be doing it and you should be doing something else.

"Dump the guilt and the superwoman syndrome," Deirdre Prescott of Silverbridge Advisors says, "Admit that you can't do everything, and that it is okay not to do everything. Men have no problem being selfish, and women should learn from them." Being selfish and knowing what is in your self interest is an essential part of keeping that oxygen mask on your own face and maintaining your strength.

In short, as Brigitte Muehlmann, a noted tax expert told me, women strive to serve, men strive for power. Women should strive for power so that they can get into a position where they can make a difference and serve better.

MARKET YOURSELF

Marketing should be a lifestyle. Give out those business cards. Talk the talk. Make promotion part of your daily routine, something that is always on your mind. Stay alert, always looking for new outlets. When you do something

"You may be disappointed if you fail, but you are doomed if you don't try." — BEVERLY SILLS

great, find a way to get the word out. Get acknowledged for it and let that acknowledgement be known. Whether you are in the public, non-profit or entrepreneurial sector, it is important to market yourself continually. Successful men and women know that.

Make sure that you have a web presence and that you update it regularly with articles, clips, notes and news. Letting your website get stale will work against you. Any time I come across one where the "recent events" are more than three months old, I have a feeling the business is not doing all that well.

Put together a list of your writing, your speaking engagements or any attention you have received in the press. If that is not at the level that you want it to be, go out and make it happen, and then put it on the web.

Trap all email addresses of contacts you meet. Get them updated and organized. Send an email blast (which is much more cost effective than regular mail) whenever something noteworthy happens. Think about sending a regular – perhaps monthly - email blast to your contacts containing news in your field that you would like them to know, or just summarizing your thoughts on a prominent topic.

When you are communicating in a targeted way with one person for a specific reason, a good strategy is to send both email and a handwritten note. The email can say that "a snail mail note is on its way but in the meantime…." The reason for both is that the person will then have your email and contact information and may immediately respond. Sending a handwritten note on nice stationary formalizes the connection and makes a statement that you care more than just shooting off the quick email. It also acts as a reminder if the person has not yet responded to your email.

With new business development in mind, spend an hour a day on marketing yourself, your firm, business or organization. Figure out what your distinguishing strengths are. Do a business plan and a marketing plan each year and look at each quarter, then each month. That will force you to focus your goals.

Each year I sit down and review what I have accomplished, where new business has come from, what the most profitable business relationship is, where I needed to improve and where I want to drive forward.

Sometimes there are surprises. I do a tremendous amount of public speaking – about 36 presentations a year. I knew a significant amount of my new business was derived from those presentations. What I did not realize until I did my analysis was that the new business did not come from the audience participants, but rather from co-panelists. In retrospect it made sense. The relationship that I built with the co-panelists is much stronger through the planning and partnering process than is the relationship developed with the audience in an hour-long presentation.

The lesson from that analysis was that I should never give another presentation by myself, but rather always give a presentation as part of a team of qualified persons who are also compatible referral sources.

If you are working in an organization and want to advance, you need to market yourself internally. Your most important "clients" are those in positions of authority in the organization. Make a concerted effort to increase your visibility. Make your accomplishments known to those who have influence. This should be done, of course with the right mix of sophistication and aggression. Developing savvy self promotion allows perception to become reality.

BRAND YOURSELF

When running for office, politicians take the time to brand themselves and execute on that brand in short order. Very quickly you understand who they are and what their strengths are. They make conscious decisions as to how they want to be come across and then make it happen.

You can do that too. How does the world perceive you? How do you want to be perceived? What do you stand for and how can you demonstrate it by your image and your actions? This should be a conscious decision.

The Jackie Kennedy White House costume exhibit in New York City offered surprising insight into the concept of branding. Every outfit she wore, every color she chose, had a purpose. She knew where she was going – to whom she would be speaking and what mattered in the country and to that head of state. She did her homework and used her clothes as a backdrop in her message. That was part of the brand. Branding does not have to be overt. It just has to make sense and coincide with your image.

SAY THANK YOU

When people send you clients or give your name to someone who is beneficial for you to know, acknowledge the effort. Call or send them a handwritten note. Let them know that the loop has been closed and you have been in the process of being interviewed or been retained.

PLAY OUTSIDE THE BOX

For those of us who can articulate anything, argue any position and convince ourselves verbally of whatever we want to hear, a nice exercise is to stop talking and start drawing. That brings another part of the brain to the problem-solving party. In addition to lists and goal setting I now also draw maps.

To determine who was giving me clients and why, for example, I bought a large poster board and magic markers. First I wrote down my most significant client relationships. Then I back tracked, remembering the connections that brought each of those clients to my door - who introduced me to them, where they came from.

I drew arrows and lines to visualize relationships, and it led to an amazing conclusion: Most of my biggest clients came from connections that originated with only three people I have known for at least 15 years – talk about a visualization. To me that underscored the value of those relationships, and I do not think I would have otherwise intuited how important they were.

It also made me understand that the 80/20 rule (the principle that in any situation, 20% of the people are responsible for 80% of the results) happens with relationships too.

After I saw how rewarding and enlightening this exercise was, I began to visually map out goals too. If I wanted to increase penetration in a certain geographic area or through a certain center of influence, then I would buy a poster board and put the names of everyone I could think of, whether I had met them or not, on that pasteboard. Then with a different color marker I linked the people I thought knew each other - or who I thought should know each other - together.

It is a different and effective way to explore and expand your mind.

Be creative with your marketing too. In 2004 I wrote a book, *Women & Money: A Practical Guide to Estate Planning*. Once it was in hand the question became, how do I market it? For me, presenting seminars was a natural fit, and I approached those with compatible practices with the possibility of presenting a seminar.

The head of an accounting firm and I presented an estate planning seminar for women. We invited a well known master chef to cook dinner after the presentation and advertised that on the invitation, knowing that the women would come because of the chef. That would be the hook to get them to listen to us.

We put tremendous thought into whom we invited to attend, made sure each table had a current client of each of ours, a prospective client of each of ours, and an employee of each of our firms whose specialty was compatible with the client and prospect. We briefed his employees on what to expect and what we expected as an outcome. We made sure each woman walked away with a gift bag that included flowers, a bottle of wine and my book. The event was a tremendous success, and both of us attracted new business because of the way it was handled.

A local hospital that had just opened a breast care center, thought *Women and Money* would be a perfect topic for a fundraiser. We invited 100 women to lunch, charging each $50.00 to attend, and that check was written out to the new breast care center at the hospital. The event was a triple win – the breast care center was highlighted and met new donors, my book was highlighted, and the women had a wonderful time.

CRACK THE $$ CODE
STRATEGIES TO DECIPHER THE CODE

Go for the "A" and earn what you are worth.

Understand your value; Do not undervalue your services or contribution.

Good is often good enough; most of the time perfection is not necessary

Ask for it! Getting what you want and what you are worth is your responsibility - no one else's.

"No" is an acceptable word in your vocabulary - use it.

Delegate, delegate, delegate. If someone under you can do the project you are working on, then delegate it and work on something that is important for you to do.

Market Yourself. Get out there and hustle.

Brand Yourself. Examine how you are perceived and compare it to the brand you want to establish for yourself.

Play Outside the Box; be creative and figure out how to maximixe your value.

CODE No. 2 Set Goals

TOO MANY WOMEN START OFF IN THEIR CAREERS, THEIR BUSINESSES OR their jobs without a compass or a plan. They don't know where they want to end up, and they don't chart their course to achieve what they want. Successful men always have goals they are not afraid to state. ("I intend to be the number one salesman." "I intend to make one million dollars." "I intend to be the best in the region, and here is how I am going to do that.").

Steve Scott, author of *Mentored by a Millionaire and Master Strategies of SuperAcheivers* points out that if you were leaving on a two week cross country vacation to a destination you had never driven to before, you would never consider taking the trip without consulting a map or at least taking one with you. Knowing you only have a limited amount of time you would want to make the vacation the best possible vacation. You would pick the destination in advance, study the various routes and select the ones that met your goal for an enjoyable, efficient trip.

Once you start on your journey, you would continually check your progress because you really value the time off from work and the opportunity it affords you and your family to have a great time together. As Mr. Scott points out, even though no one would ever start a vacation without first determining her destination and using a map to reach it, 97% of all adults drive through life without clearly defining their desired destinations and following a map to reach them.

Even worse, they let circumstances and other people dictate where they go and when to change their direction. How sad that all of those people take the time and effort to determine their destinations, routes and plans for their vacations, but miss the opportunities to fulfill their dreams for the other 50 weeks of the year, year in and year out. The ability to set goals effectively is a skill we all have and most of us underuse.

If you don't know where you are going, that is exactly where you will end up. The key is always to keep in mind the big picture, the long term goals. Set daily, weekly, monthly and annual goals. Decide what categories of your life, including your career, are important to you and then make a preliminary decision as to where you want to end up three years from now. Once you start to focus on that, it will become clear that you cannot be there without breaking that goal down into short term goals and sub tasks. Creating a business plan for your life and taking those goals and tasks seriously – reviewing, following up and revising them continuously – can lead to amazing results.

My personal goal setting system starts with three year goals, then narrows down to annual goals, quarterly goals, weekly goals and daily tasks. These goals are in the areas that mean the most to me – relationships with family, sense of purpose, health, financial achievement, professional success, and spirituality.

It does not matter what goals (and underlying tasks) you select. What matters is that you consistently review and revise them. Ben Franklin was a master at that; he set regular goals, spent significant time focusing on his strengths and weaknesses and analyzed his progression in his journals.

Focusing on the goals and tasks and moving to the next step in an organized but non rigid way leads to tremendous leaps in attainment of those goals. I schedule an annual, quarterly and monthly goal and task review dates in my calendar. Each Sunday night I spend about 30 minutes, reviewing, prioritizing and breaking down goals and tasks for the upcoming week and follow up on the prior week's goals to makes sure that they are next accomplished.

Each morning I spend at least fifteen minutes reviewing the goals and tasks at hand – leading up to the bigger picture, and then coming back down again with three specific tasks (sometimes big, sometimes small) to accomplish that day. I try very hard to achieve those goals and yet set realistic expectations. If I don't make them, I roll them to the next day. If I don't accomplish all the goals and tasks in a given week I roll them to the next week. Looking at the same goal over and over again leads to its completion.

Examples of goals could include (and it is important for each goal to set a realistic date by which you commit to its completion):

I. ANNUAL FINANCIAL GOALS

A. This year's annual income – January 1. Starting point. December 31st. End Goal

i. Base income/Salary
ii. Investment income
iii. Other business income (rental real estate, other business interests)
iv. Other earned income – royalty income, speaking income

B. Target Net worth at end of year vs

Net Worth as of beginning of year
Target Net Worth at end of year
Assets that will be acquired
Assets that will be sold
Amount of income that will be reinvested in assets/business – proportion, source and goals.
Beginning debt
Targeted debt reduction

C. Savings/Investments

Amount in savings investments at beginning of year vs. target amount at end of year.
Monthly addition target amount.
Allocation of new additions and current investments.

D. Business Enterprises

Launch of new, related business enterprise.
Business Plan Completion Target Date
Marketing Plan Completion Target Date
Establish informal board of advisors
Develop mission statement.
Start up capital – how much do you need and how are you going to obtain it
Start up expenses – rent, utilities, staff. What are you going to expend and what are your options – share space, collaborate, rent, length of lease etc.
First quarter goals
Second quarter goals
Third quarter goals
Fourth quarter goals

DON'T LET THE WORLD LEAD YOU.

We live in a time where life is whizzing right by. We are assaulted with infor-mation. With the handheld Blackberry technology there is an expectation that you will and should respond to every request and inquiry instantly and 24/7. When you watch the news on TV, you notice that the commentator is speaking on a topic and there is a news banner running at the bottom of the screen on another topic. When you sit at your computer email alerts flash in "breaking news" (most of which is, of course, not breaking at all.)

In the midst of the constant barrage and immediate expectations we all face it is a real effort to step back and remember that it is important to be proactive – that instead of having all that is coming at you control your time and thoughts, it is up to you to figure out what is important to you to achieve, prioritize it and achieve it.

Take the time to set, revise and review your goals. Once you start to achieve your goals and set new ones, your success will accelerate as the world opens up – it can't not.

"Until you value yourself, you won't value your time. Until you value your time, you will not do anything with it" —M. SCOTT PECK

CRACK THE $$ CODE
STRATEGIES TO DECIPHER THE CODE

Determine where you are on the map.

Set your destination. Where do you want to go and when do you plan to get there?

Plan the steps to get there.

Spend time each day reviewing, revising and accomplishing goals.

When you attain your goals, set new ones.

Shoot for the moon; you will land in the stars.

CODE
No. **3** Get a
Contract

IN A MAY, 2009 *VOGUE MAGAZINE* ARTICLE MODEL PAULINA PRIZKOVA
interviewed Lauren Hutton on what it was like being a model in 1975. Lauren said she modeled by the hour back then. A good working model would have six jobs a day. "You'd get a dollar a minute, $60 an hour. If you worked for Vogue you were getting $70 for the whole day. So when the Revlon thing came along, suddenly I was no longer getting $60 an hour. I was getting $25,000 a day, and that was shocking."

Paulina asked how that happened. Lauren replied that she read a New York Times article about baseball pitcher Catfish Hunter in which he said he was going to get a million dollar contract because he had to do it, since he was in a youth-oriented business.

"I was either 31 or about to turn 31," Lauren said. "Veruschka had retired; Twiggy had retired; Jean Shrimpton had retired. All the stars were gone. Dick Avedon had no choice but to work with me continually. I yelled over to my boyfriend and asked 'How do you get a contract?'

"He didn't even take a second to yell back: 'Don't tell them. Don't do any makeup ads. Just refuse to do it. Tell all your photographers you want a contract.' Avedon got it like that, and after six months, that was it."

"So for six months you did not do anything?" Pauline asked.

"I worked all day," Lauren answered, "I was always triple booked. Just no cosmetic ads. It took six months to work out a contract that had never been worked out before, and basically all contracts were based on that."

When you enter into a contract with another party you are taking that business relationship to a more formal level. It can be a very effective exercise for you as a woman, because it forces you to write down in black and white what you think you are worth and how you are going to get paid.

If you have your own business and are sending out contracts to customers, those terms set the value. For women who may tend to undervalue themselves, sending written contracts out minimizes that risk, as the financial terms are already in the hands of the potential customer, and it is then a lot harder to undercut the price they themselves have set.

DO THE RESEARCH

When negotiating a contract, the first step is to figure out what you are worth to the person or company you are negotiating with. If you are already in your current job and want to enter into a contract or renew a contract, you can't look at what you would be earning if you were working somewhere else. (If that is your goal, then go work somewhere else.) Instead, do your homework and find out how others are being compensated in similar positions where you are, and more importantly, how a new lateral hire coming in to a similar position is being compensated. It may be that base pay is pretty similar across the board, but the timing of the payments, the determination of the bonus, the additional perks all may vary significantly.

Ask the open questions in your research: What are the available benefits and who has them? Is there anything else I should be considering? Are there benefits I am unaware of? Is there flexibility on the timing of the payments?

Spend some significant time figuring out what you want to negotiate for and prioritizing it. In doing this research, quite frankly, it helps to ask men what they think. Lauren Hutton's boyfriend had a quick answer. He did not have to think about it. I have found that to be universally true. Developing a kitchen cabinet of successful men and women will be invaluable.

It is also important to hire an attorney and an accountant – if possible people who negotiate the legal and economic terms of similar persons in your field and therefore are aware of the different types of clauses that would go into the contracts and ball park fee ranges. That does not mean you have to follow the given advice; it means that you can use that research in figuring out how you want to negotiate.

PLAN AHEAD IN ESTABLISHING VALUE

About fifteen years ago I was involved with a client in the negotiation of the purchase of a major league sports team. The agent who was instrumental in the deal told me a very valuable piece of advice, something we all know but I don't think most women would instinctively think of. He said, "When you are entering a contract, you have to set the value at the beginning. You only make big money twice – when you enter a contract and when you leave. All in the middle is just maintenance."

I have thought about that advice a lot. You cannot enter into a contract for $150,000 a year and then think that you will be able to earn your way up to $250,000 a year. That would be very difficult to do because you set the value proposition at $150,000 and unless that additional $100,000 or the mechanism for obtaining it is somehow built into that initial contract, no employer or business colleague is going to decide that you are worth the extra $100,000 without your bringing a very significant increase in the value to the table, and that just doesn't happen very frequently and should not be relied on.

Something else to remember: It is okay to renegotiate. Most women who search for the "A" and strive to be the best they can be, when and if they finally sign a contract, look at that as an end goal. Men, on the other hand instinctively know that all contracts can be renegotiated and that the signing of a contract is a beginning point, not the end point.

For that reason, you may wish to consider the length of the contract. My feeling is that most contracts should be of three year duration – especially if they are for significant sums. That is because it takes a least a year to figure out how to achieve the results and get the lay of the land, at least a year to show your performance, and it could take a year to renegotiate the contract for better terms.

As Bonnie Brown Hartley, a very successful family business consultant says, when trying to figure out how to determine fees for a project, whether you charge by the hour, the day or the project, remember that if you undercharge initially you will ultimately either lose money or resent the contract.

Do your homework. Find out the range of fees others in your field charge. Create a spreadsheet of all known expenses, including your time. If you have to travel to do the work, factor for that time too. You don't need to add the travel time on as an extra charge but you do have to understand the value of your time and the cost of travel if you choose not to charge for it.

Many women are shy about negotiating for themselves and uncomfortable being their own advocate, but there is simply no other course. Learning to overcome the shyness and discomfort is something you really need to do. Once you have done the research, only you know the terms and conditions that are right for you in setting the stage for this phase of your life.

Take that first step and start advocating for yourself now.

CREATE YOUR OWN REVIEW

This is also true in your existing job/career. In most positions as an employee you are "reviewed" on an annual basis. That is when you are called in and your strengths, weaknesses and areas of improvement are summarized. You are told where you stand, and often this review is tied to your compensation/bonus/career track. Many women make this a one-way process. They expect to be judged, and they listen to what is said.

A better idea is to take the time in advance to review all your accomplishments and write them down. After all, who knows better than you what you are doing and what value you bring to the organization?

In one of my first associate positions I knew that I was going to be reviewed, and I was pretty sure no one understood what I had accomplished, so I put together a ten page report on what I had done. The report was not just a list. It had numbers in it - ways that my results had driven revenue, client relationships that had been strengthened because of my involvement, ideas and directions I had suggested. It also included a listing of ideas and strategies I was currently working on. I knew what was important to the firm, and I made sure that my report addressed all of those factors and my contributions.

The managing partner and committee were taken aback by the amount of work I had put into it. They told me they had never seen anything like that. At the end of the report I asked for a certain dollar bonus, and I received it. I later found out that the bonus I asked for was the highest bonus given to any associate that year.

Setting and achieving goals may be difficult to do on your own. Sometimes the right thing to do is to hire a coach.

As executive coach Cynthia Adams Harrison of Thomas Davidow & Associates notes, like athletic coaches in sports, the goal of executive coaches in business is to enhance performance by identifying and limiting both in-

"Until the contract is signed, nothing is real."
— GLENN DANZIG

ternal and external distractions. Internal distractions are those which come from within the individual, such as lack of confidence, negative thinking and anxiety - either self imposed, or aggravated by increased pressure for job performance.

External business distractions come from the environment and are primarily related to industry limits/obstacles and corporate limits. They can include a noisy or chaotic work place, unexpected events, a lack of financial, technical or personnel resources, a manager who is non-communicative or hostile, compensatory practices, organizational constructs/designs, the cultural and political environment and goal orientation.

Good executive coaches develop an understanding of the system you are working in and then create interventions which help you achieve your goals.

CRACK THE $$ CODE
STRATEGIES TO DECIPHER THE CODE

Contracts matter; their formality establishes value.

Do the research. What should the terms of a contract be?

Ask the open questions. What else should you be negotiating for?

Hire the right professionals to give you expert advice from their vantage points.

Put together your informal board of advisors - friends and colleagues - and ask for advice.

Establish the value proposition; what would you be willing to enter the contract for and what would you be willing to exit the contract for?

Create your own review. Don't rely on others to determine your value. Figure out yourself what you have accomplished before your performance is reviewed.

Stick up for yourself; you should not expect anyone else to do that for you.

Renegotiate your contract when you feel that you deserve more.

CODE No. 4 Partnering is Key

GOOD PARTNERS CREATE MAGIC. BAD PARTNERS CAUSE EXTREME DISRUP-tion. While women know that is true in their personal lives, they often don't realize it is true in their professional lives too. Steve Scott, the multimillionaire entrepreneur/author says, "The single greatest strategy in achieving success is to partner up with people who can help you with things you are clueless about."

As Dune Thorne of Silverbridge Advisors stresses, even though your instinct may be to hire and partner with those who share your strengths, it is imperative that you make it a priority to find partners and employees whose strengths are your weaknesses. Don't be afraid to hire or partner with those who are better than you. It will only make you improve. Long term success is tied to the quality and caliber of the people you choose to partner with.

WHAT QUALITIES COMPLEMENT YOURS?

Before deciding on a professional partner, you need to take the time to evaluate your strengths and weaknesses. Ask others what they think – your spouse, your children, your parents, your best friends. You will be amazed at the commonality of the answers, and it may jump start your analysis of the type of partners you will need to compensate for your weaknesses.

If you are an extroverted sales person who likes to close a sale and move on, maybe the right partner is the back office finance person or the steadfast assistant who completes the paperwork. If you had someone else (hourly, part time or full time) to accomplish those tasks, wouldn't that make you more productive and help you focus on what you excel at?

If you are an introverted technician who likes to write or perform technical tasks and does not enjoy selling or networking, perhaps the right partner for you is a marketing/public relations genius who can help you put your materials in the right business-savvy venues in a way that is comfortable for you.

A WISE AND TRUSTED COUNSELOR CAN HELP

Rhoda Weinman, an accomplished attorney tells of the early stage of her career in the mid 1980s at a Fortune 500 company. She plugged away with persistence doing what she thought was the right next step to advance. However, her career did not take off like a rocket until a partner in the firm took notice of her capabilities, guided her career path and helped her navigate her way through the corporate culture. Under her mentor's watchful eye she was promoted several times and ultimately was hired for a prize managerial position. She knew she was qualified for the position; she also knew she would not have achieved it without her mentor's guidance.

Because of her mentor's support the company paid for her to go to law school. She earned her law degree and ended up with a position in the company's law department. Rhoda did not forget the importance of being mentored and made it a point for all the remaining years she worked in the company to find qualified women and help mentor them and help them build their careers.

Mentors who care about you and your success will tell you things you would never figure out on your own. A few years ago I sat next to a well known TV legal commentator/author, and I asked him about his career transitions and success. He told me that a network asked him to comment whenever certain cases came up. He did so and was very good at it. He went to the station director and told him he wanted his own show where he could showcase the commentary he was providing at a deeper level. He knew he could do it and tried hard to prove his case.

The station director told him he was not known enough, and the worst thing the station director could do for him would be to give him his own show. Instead the station director gave him a regular slot on a well watched show,

"The way a team plays as a whole determines its success. You may have the greatest bunch of individual stars in the world, but if they don't play together, the club won't be worth a dime."

— BABE RUTH

a strategic move that enabled him to build his name and his brand. He then wrote several books and one of them became a bestseller because his name recognition was now significant.

It is also important to find mentors, partners and coaches who may not be in your immediate world. Create a support system or kitchen cabinet of trusted friends whom you can talk to and bounce ideas off. Some of those people may be people you pay – executive or life coaches, lawyers or accountants. Others may be people who are trying to figure it out too and are striving to get to that next level. If you are fortunate, some of those will be people who right now run circles around you.

STRATEGIC MENTORS

Just as it would be foolish to sit and wait for Prince Charming to ride up on the white horse, so it is foolish to sit and wait for the right mentor to tap you on the shoulder because you have been sitting at your desk doing a good job. Look around strategically and figure out whom you should choose to be your mentor and develop a plan to make that happen.

Is there someone ahead of you in your career whom you would like to model? Find a way to meet that person. Maybe start off with an email and ask advice.

ACCIDENTAL MENTORS

About fifteen years ago one of my bosses (a woman) was going on vacation and asked me to cover a speaking engagement. I had not done much public speaking before, and this was an important client for the firm. I agreed and agonized over how to prepare.

I gave the five speeches and received rave reviews. It turned out the reviews were actually too good. The client called me and said from that point forward he wanted me, not my boss, to make future presentations. I was horrified and did not know what to do. My boss was still on vacation and so I went to the managing partner of the firm, explained what had happened and told the managing partner that I was not comfortable with this. I did not want to hurt my boss's feelings, and I did not want to outshine my boss. I did not want to do the future speaking engagements and I did not know what to do.

He told me that I had no choice but to do it, because at this point if I turned it down, it was likely that the firm would lose the client. When my boss returned from vacation, I was a nervous wreck, and when I spoke to my boss, I explained the situation. My boss was magnanimous and told me that meant I must be an excellent speaker and launched me on my speaking career. For more than fifteen years (long after we stopped working together) that boss has supported my endeavors and opened up new opportunities to me.

VIRTUAL MENTORS

Are there people you don't know personally who are accomplished and have a marketing presence or website? If so, study it. How are they developing their business? Are they giving seminars, presentations, writing books, writing articles? What is their focus? Does it shift? How do they communicate with their prospects? How do they ask their prospects/clients to communicate with them? What is their brand? What is their message? Do they have any awards? What organizations do they belong to? What leadership roles do they take on? Identify a few "virtual mentors' and track them to watch their progress.

Develop an organized system of tracking who they are, where they are and what is important to them. Good sales people know how to do this.

GATHER SUPPORTERS

Many women believe if you present the facts - the evidence coupled with a strong, sound argument - you'll win over the boardroom. Provide some information ahead of time, let people digest it, present your case, and if it makes sense for the company, they'll approve it. However, if you have a committee or board you are answering to or leading and an important vote is up, you cannot rely on truth and justice prevailing.

Men seem to instinctively know this and tend to be more politically astute. They understand that boardroom decisions require behind-the-scenes action first.

Let's go for political astuteness. Figure out your constituents – those who will support you no matter what, those with whom you need to build support for your initiatives and objectives, those who will make their decisions based entirely on facts, and those who may or may not support you but are influential at the table with others, and thus their buy-in is vital. (It wouldn't hurt also to know those who will probably never be of assistance or support, for whatever reasons.)

It is important to "count your votes" and understand before an important vote how the members will be voting.

Have the right conversations with the committee/board members prior to the vote so that they are prepared and can handle it. Any vote that happens should not be a surprise ambush. Think through how to handle the outcome of the meeting and whether or not knowing how it turns out would lead to a change in your thought process.

FRIENDSHIPS AND BUSINESS

Women excel in building relationships and developing good connections, but men know how to use those connections more effectively. For women making connections satisfies an emotional need, and if a woman is not careful, the creation of the connection and the maintenance of the relationship can become the end goal.

Men know that the creation of the connection is just the starting gate, and that it is okay to take that connection, build the relationship and ride it to business success. Men understand that a good working relationship is something they must foster and keep working on. They understand that although they don't know when they may "need" that contact in the future, it will prove useful. The contact may refer friends and business associates to them at any time for any reason. Women are more reluctant to "use" their relationships for business purposes.

Abby Slater, an entrepreneur who has done a great deal of work raising money for charities, also notes that any time she asked a man to help her with raising money and sharing his contacts, he did it. In other words, if the man gave $100, that would be important. If he gave $100 and introduced her to six

"Self-esteem isn't everything; it's just that there's nothing without it." — GLORIA STEINAM

others who gave some dollar amount, there was real leverage in that. Business is based on reciprocity.

In most cases, however, whenever she made the same request of women, they gave money to the charity personally but did not involve others they knew in the ask. To the women giving money was itself enough – broadening and deepening the circle - and giving more was not an instinct.

However, you owe more to those who give more. That means, of course, that you have to be careful whom you ask. You should only want to create reciprocal relationships with those you feel comfortable giving back to. If you develop relationships with people you do not feel comfortable being reciprocal with, you will put yourself in a box. You will feel obligated to give back because someone gave to you, but you will also be conflicted about what that means.

I learned that lesson the hard way. In the early days of starting my career, I took business from anyone who wanted to give it to me. It did not occur to me to differentiate. It became clear, after a while, that not everyone was on the same playing field – some times in terms of competence, other times, integrity. If you take a client or business from someone who is not playing the game the way you do, that person will expect you to send something back, and in life your reputation is what is most important. If you cannot reciprocate the relationship don't enter into it.

It seems that men "know the rules" and understand building connections with reciprocity. They know that if you ask someone to donate money to your charity, there will be a reciprocal ask happening, and that it is okay; that is part of the relationship-building process. Men tend to view a relationship as something that has both personal and business aspects.

Most women connect the relationship at the personal level, and asking for money or a contribution is trickier and harder to do. They are more likely to separate out the personal and business aspects of relationships and have the personal part lead. For a woman to ask a friend or neighbor whom she knows on a personal level for business means crossing a boundary and changing the relationship. I have noticed that relationships that started off as business relationships in my life can easily turn to include friendship, but friendship relationships do not easily turn to include business. That is distinctly female; men jump back and forth across that boundary with ease.

Why? Is it because we fear doing business together will hurt the friendship? Because we have a different value for friends than we do for clients? Because we are uncomfortable charging friends for services? Because we are less comfortable discussing money than men are?

Whatever the reason, we are losing out. I have had to push myself to cross that boundary line a few times in my life - and when I have, I have been surprised at how significant the rewards have been. A good friend of mine is general counsel in a law department for a Fortune 100 corporation. He is responsible for assigning contract work to lawyers. Part of how I am compensated depends (as with any lawyer in a law firm) on how much business I bring to the firm, whether it is in my field or not. I knew that this friend thought well of my professional skills and I knew the corporate department in our firm was excellent. I agonized about whether or not to ask, and how to do it, but finally I had to convince myself and force myself to do it. I sent him an email explaining what I wanted – an email because I was so uncomfortable asking that I just could not pick up the phone and do it.

It worked. He called me and sent a small case in. The corporate department handled it so well that it led to a procession of increasingly complex and lucrative work.

CONNECTIONS BUILD BUSINESS

Men take the importance of those connections seriously and put together a game plan on how to leverage them and make them effective. One of the first law firms I worked in had an annual Christmas party for its important clients. The lawyers in the office were hand picked. You were selected that year if you were a "star" and if you had the opportunity to increase the depth of the relationship between the firm and the clients. The managing partner of that firm took building those relationships and the money expended to make it happen very seriously. Each year on the day of the Christmas party he would call into the conference room all of the selected lawyers – most of whom were older than I was and most of whom where men – and he would remind them of the rules that were to be followed at the party: 1) No lawyer was to eat the shrimp –that was for the guests and too expensive. 2) You had to have a glass of beer or wine in your hand so that the guests felt comfortable, but you were not allowed to drink it; 3) No lawyers were to congregate and speak to each other; the point of the evening was to connect with clients. His preplanning and "lecture" worked. Every year the firm achieved new connections, strengthened existing relationships and increased revenue from the party.

Men also understand that the entire world is connected and positive connections may prove useful later on. One of the first firms I worked in had a policy that whenever an attorney left (unless that attorney was fired) there was a lunch in his or her honor where the attorney's contributions to the firm were applauded. That firm knew that it is a small world. That attorney could very well end up in a position to refer business back or to recommend someone in the firm for a position.

Women should make the effort to mentor women. I have been fortunate to have strong women (as well as male) mentors. Women should especially mentor women because men, no matter how enlightened, cannot possibly understand how hard it is to do what women have to do professionally to succeed in the workplace and what women have to do at home to keep that front stable. No matter how much men today are partnering on the home front it seems the universal truth that women still juggle more balls.

I have always remembered that, and I also have always understood that it is important to do what is right for the junior person. If a young associate comes to me and wants to leave to go to another opportunity that may be better for him or her, I remember that I did that a few times too. I was always grateful to the boss who told me that he wanted the very best for me, and I understand the importance of wanting continued success for that young associate.

Many men build their relationships by bonding outside the office – playing golf, grabbing a beer after work. An informal setting outside the office is essential to building and maintaining business relationships.

When women network with women they know how to do that and do it very well – lunch, dinner, drinks, charity events, speaking engagements. When women network with men, they have harder time thinking about that – especially when it comes to bonding with men outside the office. A safe way to do that may be luncheon meetings or maybe even an early dinner. Grabbing a beer is a lot trickier and can send mixed messages that do not enhance a woman's relationship or image.

If you can find a way to work sports in, it makes it easier. Taking male colleagues to dinner and then the baseball, football or hockey game – especially if it is a "hot" team - minimizes the risk that the invitation will be misinterpreted and provides a safe, informal, relaxed networking atmosphere. If you golf, inviting men to join you (as long as you are all at similar skill levels) can also work.

IT'S NOT PERSONAL!

Not all slights, especially those that occur in a professional setting, are intentional. Not all criticism is personal. Taking slights personally can impede or implode a relationship. Here again the sexes in general behave differently to the disadvantage of women.

Just as women are less comfortable transforming their personal relationships into business relationships, so they have more trouble turning off emotion for the sake of pragmatism. They are more likely than men to take a professional criticism personally, feel wounded by the remark, and give up on the relationship as a result.

Men, on the other hand, usually do not "sweat the small stuff", and they do not take any and every slight as a personal one. They are much more likely to "wink, nod" and stay on course, contemplating the big picture and the greater importance of maintaining the business relationship. They will shrug off a slight and have dinner the next week with the offender.

WHEN THE PARTNER IS A COACH

Playing or performing without one or more coaches is just plain foolish. If you can find partners with complementary skills, then s/he might have some areas covered, but even in the areas where you or they already excel, it's short-sighted to trust just your own eyes.

Barbara Reinhold, a talent management consultant and executive coach based in New England, works with a variety of organizations and individuals both by phone and in-person to help high-potential people perform better. According to Reinhold, a good coach will help you learn to ask yourself the questions like the following, and then get feedback from others about how well you're meeting your own goals and getting the rewards you deserve:

- What are my top 2 goals here?
- What am I doing to achieve each one?
- On a scale if 1-10, how aggressive am I being in pursuit of those two goals? If the answer is less than 8, you might want to just take it off the list, and wait until you're ready to be earning at least a B in passionate follow-through with this item. It's better to remove a goal from your list than starve it to death for lack of attention.

- How are my feelings helping me and hurting me in attaining these goals? How can I use/manage them better?
- How might I be selling myself short in terms of achieving my major goals?
- Am I remembering to put on my own oxygen mask first in this situation? How might I do that better?

Often the coaches can be peer coaches or mentors, but at various points it's also helpful to invest a little in yourself by working with a good coach who understands both you and the things you're trying to accomplish.

CRACK THE $$ CODE
STRATEGIES TO DECIPHER THE CODE

Who are the partners in your life? Are they the right ones?

Who could be other partners in your life? Do you know them? If not, how might you find them?

Analyze your strengths and weaknesses and determine who is complementary to both.

Do you have a mentor?

Who are good mentor choices?

How can you reach out to them?

Surf the web for virtual mentors?

Friends can be good partners; ask them for business.

Connections build business. Use them.

Hire a strategic or personal coach.

CODE No. 5 | Image Matters

PERCEPTION MATTERS. OPINIONS ARE FORMED IN A MATTER OF SECONDS.
Look the role in order to get the role.

I do a great deal of public speaking. In my early speaking days I presented a seminar to potential clients on Nantucket. I was there for a few days. It was in the heat of the summer, and I was casually (and coolly) dressed. A man in the audience came up to me after the presentation and said. "You did a great job presenting your material – only problem was your clothing. If you want wealthy smart people to hire you as their lawyer, when you are presenting material to them you must dress like a lawyer. Regardless of what they are wearing you should have been in a suit. They are on vacation. You are working. "And quite frankly" he added, "I think it is important whenever you are making a presentation to dress better and more professionally than your audience – whoever they are."

That was the first time that it had occurred to me that image matters in client attraction and retention, and I have never forgotten it. Recently I spoke on a panel with four other professionals. A young woman on the panel was very articulate and very underdressed. She was in a suit that did not quite fit her, and she had not taken the time to really pull herself together. As I watched her speak, noting that there was no rapport between her and the audience, I remembered what that man in Nantucket had told me. If she had been making her presentation on a speaker phone, she would have been hired by members of that audience, but her physical appearance undercut her. She did not get any new clients that day.

Of course, what field you are in and whom you are trying to attract can alter this rule. A very successful fundraiser for a major university told me that in her world it is important to look good – but not "too good". The prospective donor wants to know she is professional but she has to look as though she is not "all set". In other words, she should look comfortable but not too wealthy and appropriate for her role in asking others for money.

Five of us were recently selected as "Best Lawyers in America" – a very prestigious honor. The organization asked us to have a group photo taken that would appear in The Boston Globe and several national websites. The other four were men. It is a lot easier for them to throw on a "good suit" and walk to the shoot. For a 50 year-old-woman that just is not possible. The weekend before the shoot I took four outfits that I thought were my better ones out of my closet and had a friend take digital photos to see how they looked when photographed. Of course, the outfit I had thought would be the best was not; a different one was. I intentionally made the outfit season-less, figuring that if the photo was going on a website, it might stay there for a long time, and a summer suit would stand out to someone looking at it in December. I spent two hours in advance of that shoot having my hair and makeup done (I can't imagine how Oprah or Hillary Clinton can spend that much time each day having that done). The results were well worth it. I know when I feel better about the way it look is directly reflected in my performance, in how I perceive the world and in how it perceives me.

DRESS WITH A PURPOSE

A few years ago, as the number of my speaking presentations dramatically increased and as my media appearances became more frequent, I decided to hire an image consultant. Going through my closet with her was an eye-opening experience. She pointed out that a significant amount of the clothes in that closet were black, and that black was not a good color for me. We sorted the clothes into piles – keep, give to charity and toss. It was a very interesting exercise because somewhere along the way it became clear that I had become a "Filene's Basement" shopper – in other words I would pick up this blouse or this skirt because it had a good price and a good label, but I had no ability overall to put the pieces together in a coordinated fashion.

I had also fallen into some label traps. One in particular, I remember, was a navy St. John suit with a long jacket. I had spent a lot of money on it. It trav-

"You can have whatever you want if you dress for it." — EDITH HEAD

eled well and was very beautiful. "All well and good," she said, "but I bet you have never had anyone compliment you when you were wearing it. It does nothing for you. Your jackets should be short and cropped."

(She was right about the suit, but I was unable to part with it. It hangs in a hidden corner of my closet, even now.)

As part of that image consulting she also brought me back to colors that are right for me – earth tones, browns, greens and blues. She suggested I change my hair and my makeup. She was right across the board, and I do not think I ever could have figured that all out by myself.

Color and proper fitting clothes are critical to image success. As image consultant Diana Moore notes, building a wardrobe with the help of a trusted professional – not a girlfriend or sister- will lead to better choices that you will enjoy for years. And in the end, you will spend less as you will only purchase pieces that will suit you. With the right things in your closet you can get dressed quickly, pack for a trip easily and always be confident about your appearance. You will feel comfortable, appropriate and attractive and free to focus on the important work you do.

We all have one or two favorite outfits that make us feel pretty, powerful and pulled together. I know that for many years I would gravitate toward my favorite outfits and keep wearing them – without enough regard to which day that week or month would be the best to wear them.

Part of image strategy is to look at your calendar each week and each month and look at what your important appointment/meetings are – professional, charitable or otherwise - and strategically figure out which are the right outfits for those days. Shop in your closet, mix and match accessories. Instead of deciding what you are going to wear on a given day five minutes before you go into the shower, map it out each week and month.

You will dress better because you will have the time to figure out how accessories – scarves, jewelry, shoes, handbags - work and you will have the time to play out new combinations and then match the right outfits to the right days. You may also want to buy an expandable garment rack and each Sunday night hang up the week's worth of outfits. This does not mean you have to stick with it. It means that you will have given much more thought to it than you are doing now. It is great if you have an "eye" for putting outfits together – I know I don't. Sue Cervini, an image consultant with "The Closet Consultant" did a wonderful job of taking pictures of my clothes and making "flash cards". She took the individual pieces and put them together with other pieces and accessories to create many more outfits from the clothes I had than I ever could have dreamed of. She put together color combinations that were just not intuitive to me and really worked. Instead of buying new clothing or adding new pieces, she showed me that I had a multitude of opportunities in the closet just waiting to be put together.

As Sue Cervini points out, for women re-entering the job market clothing and image may require significant effort. Figuring out what the right image is today and what the clothes are that work in the marketplace is an exercise worth doing. A good strategy would be to identify women in the work force who are in the job you are shooting for. How do they dress? Are any of them well known? Can you find pictures of them on the Internet? It is also important to take an objective look at you hairstyle and make-up. Do they fit the image? Many times a woman will put significant effort into the clothes but not the whole package.

Re-entering the work force affords a good opportunity to look at what your image is now and make an investment in getting it to where you want it to be - with clothes, accessories, hair and make-up. If you have the financial resources, considering hiring an image consultant. If not, find a store where you are comfortable, work with the personal shopper at that store if there is one, or if not, find a salesperson with whom you can work … and get going.

Cynthia C. Gardner, a personal stylist and image consultant stresses that when you vye for a job for which you are suited make an effort to dress to enhance and illustrate your personality confidence. She finds that many women look uncomfortable because they think that there is still a 'uniform' in the work place to which they have to adhere…a basic, uninteresting suit, practical shoes and underpinning. When they wear that "uniform" they look uninspired in the lineup. It is important to be upfront and center, to understand who you are and honor the position by dressing with personality and good taste. You should not wear a suit if it's not 'you'. Instead, wear a wonderful dress and interesting jewelry that lets your personality shine however, does not distract from or overwhelm you. Wearing an ensemble in which you feel comfortable is the sign of confidence. If you feel confident in your expression, whether on stage, at the anchor desk, on camera or at the podium, you will 'perform' to her utmost and your clothing will be a palpable part of a beautiful, authoritative presentation.

The image analysis reminded me of 25 years ago when I was starting out and single. When I went to a presentation coach to analyze the way I was speaking and presenting myself he was very blunt. "You keep flipping your hair and batting your eyes, and I am really confused. Are you looking for a man or a client? Get your signals straight. If you want a client from this type of presentation, then act like a professional. Dress the part, look the part and act the part. The confused image will not lead to your getting hired."

As image consultant Ginger Burr notes, knowledge is power. Understanding the statement you are making by your visual presence is critical. Then, at least, you are making an educated decision on whether to conform to a particular industry's dress code or buck the system – either way you will be prepared for the response you will get.

Image is more than personal appearance and style. You are also judged by the way you present yourself in the written word and how you interact with others. Give people what they want. It is important to show respect to those with whom you want to create a relationship. If someone refers to you by your first name, do the same in kind. If someone refers to you as "Mrs.", "Dr." or a similarly formal salutation – whether by email or by written correspondence - do the same. That keeps you on an even playing field and shows respect.

I reviewed an email a friend of mine wrote to express her desire to re-enter the job force. It was written in a very casual style without punctuation or capitalization. I told her that if that email was sent to me I would never hire her – that she was college educated and corresponding as an adolescent. Manners still matter.

SYMBOLS MATTER

A very accomplished woman I know received a significant job promotion and was offered the "corner office." She called her kitchen cabinet of men and asked them if she should take it. One of the men she called said to her, "No man would ever ask that question. A man would know he was entitled to it and that symbols matter."

Window offices and proximity to the power corridor matter. In every office there is a cluster of offices where the most powerful people in that organization work. That is an expensive neighborhood, and having your office near it matters. It means that the most powerful people can easily watch you, and it means that you can watch them. Out of sight, out of mind.

Sometimes there are conflicting symbols – window offices and power corridors. I have seen people make the mistake of picking a window office over a less prestigious office in the power corridor. Don't do that.

SEEMINGLY SMALL DETAILS MATTER

Your level of professional respect is determined (at least in part) by your title. Your title should be part of your contract negotiation. Should you change jobs, the title you had in your prior job reflects to a certain extent your competence level among your peers. Titles are never as important as dollars, but they matter.

If you have your own business, it matters what the reading materials are in the reception area. It matters how your receptionist answers the phone. It matters whether you serve a client food on a paper or china plate. You set your image by the symbols you display. It matters if you have family pictures in your office. It matters what is on the walls. All of those symbols show the person who is observing you how you think of yourself.

CRACK THE $$ CODE
STRATEGIES TO DECIPHER THE CODE

What is the image you want to present?

Is that the image you do present?

Ask others what your image is. Do their opinions reflect what you think your image is?

Have a friend take pictures of you. Look at your hair, makeup, clothes. Is this the image you want to project?

Dress with a purpose... Why are you wearing that?

Organize your wardrobe and outfits each week. Match power days with power outfits.

Symbols Matter - What is your title? Where is your office?

Seemingly small details matter.

Be yourself; Don't be afraid to have flair and style.

Hire an image consultant.

CODE No. 6 | Take Risks

A WOMAN'S INNATE DESIRE TO BE PROTECTED AND HER INSTINCT TO PROTECT others can make it very scary to take a risk.

There are financial risks. You may have to spend money before you are ready to, and that can be scary. In practical terms you may have to make a financial investment in yourself (renting an office, having business cards made) before you have revenue coming in. You may decide that you can't advance without another degree, and that means taking on debt.

It is important to evaluate the risks and the possible outcomes before proceeding and really self evaluate to decide if fear alone is what is stopping you, or if there is a valid business reason for not proceeding. If it is just fear, forge ahead and do it anyway.

Men know that turbulence is turbulence, not crashing. When women hit turbulence, they second guess their own ability to make it. Men put their seat belts on and ride through it – sometimes becoming more aggressive while in the turbulence.

RESIST THE URGE TO SPLURGE

Many women who are starting off tend to spend money as soon as they earn it. They are working hard, and they want the trappings that go along with it – good clothes, good vacations, and good handbags.

I know. I fell right into that trap. When I started working, I worked very, very hard – long hours. My pay was good, but, quite frankly, not great. And every weekend my best friend and I would take a long walk to a luxury mall and spend a lot of our paychecks on clothes and accessories. We felt good when we did it, and we felt we deserved it. It took a long time to break that habit and even longer to pay off all that credit card debt. I wish I had been more disciplined and understood the power of compounding much earlier than I did.

If you get into debt (credit card or any other kind) the interest and penalties you pay will end up being far more than what you originally borrowed. If you invest wisely, the interest, dividends and growth in that investment that you earn will be far more than what you originally invested.

If instead of investing you borrow money and do not pay it back, or you borrow money for no good reason, then you are doubling your problems by both adding to the amount you have to pay back and by losing the financial growth that would have occurred if you had prudently invested those funds.

I took a major step forward when I began to be paid significant bonuses and broke those bonuses down into categories – *spend, splurge* and *invest*. I found it very helpful to have a portion that always went to *splurge,* and I have to admit that even today there is a part of the reward for a job well done that still makes me spend some on splurge. As I have gotten older, I have added the category of philanthropy, so now when there is a significant bonus, the categories are, *spend, splurge, invest* and *give.*

INVEST IN YOURSELF

For many women making good money is an end goal; for many men making good money is the starting gate. An accomplished woman who was very senior in a major financial institution told me that she made significant money during her career, as did the men who worked next to her. After she retired, she was out to dinner with several of them and they were discussing their net worth. That was when she realized that even though they had all made the same amount of money, they had totally different thoughts about what to do with their earnings. It had never occurred to her that making that money could be the first step toward creating significant wealth. She had invested her money wisely, and it had grown. They had invested theirs in other businesses, in real estate, in partnerships. Their goal with their incomes was to create wealth. Her goal with her income was to preserve it.

The quantum leap in wealth creation does not come from what you earn, but rather what you do with what you earn. If you are not wise with it and run into debt, your net worth will crater. If you bank it, your wealth will be preserved. If you make good business decisions and have as a goal the creation of additional wealth, you may very well achieve that.

RISKS AND REWARDS

It also helps to think about your career as a business endeavor, even if that is not a typical way to approach what you are doing. That's what started Oprah's quantum leap up. In the early days she was a television host who was a paid employee on a station-owned show. She was business-savvy enough to buy the production rights and own her show. It was the ownership of her show that ramped up her net worth. Without that move she may very well have remained a very accomplished and salaried employee.

Marcy Carsey is a television producer who values independence. "When you share your financial risk with a studio," she says, "you give them part of your creative control too." She and her partner, Tom Warner, produced *The Cosby Show, Roseanne, 3rd Rock from the Sun,* and *That 70's Show.*

In the building phase of her career she was hired by Michael Eisner, the then-president of ABC and was in charge of popular shows like *Mork & Mindy* and *Soap.* She decided she did not want to run the television division of a studio and did not want to work at another network. She felt the only way for her to get ahead was to start an independent production company, even though doing so was a risk. She lured Tom Warner away from ABC, and together they formed Carsey-Warner Productions. She did everything she had to do to get their first big hit - *The Cosby Show* - on the air, including mortgaging her home and leaving her family in L.A. to go to New York to produce it, as Cosby stipulated that is where the show had to be taped. Taking financial and personal risks while backing that show and syndicating it led to extreme wealth for Carsey-Warner.

A male friend of mine tells the story of the beginning of his business. While he was a graduate student he opened a copy center inside the library of a major university by leasing space from the library. (This was long before copy centers were on every corner.) He leased a copy machine and had it delivered to the university. The company mistakenly thought that the university was leasing the machine and did not ask for credit references.

About six months after starting his business, he was struggling to make the lease payments. The leasing company came to him, found out that he was a student and was flabbergasted. They were even more flabbergasted when he told them that he figured out the only way to make the lease payments was if they leased him a second machine so he could increase production. He showed them the financial analysis, spreadsheets and marketing analysis.

They agreed with him, leased him the second machine (as the only way to recoup their money) and within a year he made a significant amount of money from the contracts.

Barbara Reinhold, author of *"Free to Succeed: Designing the Life You Want in The New Free Agent Economy"* speaks of "multiple streams of income", how, in addition to your "day job", you might also think about creative ways to increase cash flow from alternative sources – freelance writing, consulting, etc. Having those alternative streams of income can be particularly helpful in a downturn economy because they keep cash coming in if disaster strikes.

If a goal is to create wealth, you cannot think the way an employee would; you have to think outside the box and be very creative about the ways to approach the creation of wealth.

It is also important, as Kenny Roger sings, to "know when to fold 'em". Be sensitive to the signs of adversity and quit before it's too late when a business venture seems to be going sour. If, however, your career or job is not working for you, if you are not happy, if you are in stress every day, then do something about it. Take that risk and make the switch.

If you can't figure out on your own what you want to do, hire a coach or ask your friends. Go out and start informational interviews. Find your passion and take the risk of going for it, no matter what it is. Oprah Winfrey has made a significant living by talking with people and sharing real experiences. No matter what you want to do, there is a way to do it. It is up to you to put the plan in place, figure it out and then take the risk.

BETTER TO ASK FORGIVENESS THAN PERMISSION

Sometimes it is worth the risk to take the initiative and assert leadership, even if you don't have the authorization to do so. Often a situation is in desperate need of leadership but there is no clear authoritative figure. Take a chance and fill the vacuum.

A good friend of mine graduated from dental school and wanted to start

"I dream, I test my dreams against my beliefs, I dare to take risks, and I execute my vision to make those dreams come true." — WALT DISNEY

her own business. She worried that her husband would be opposed to it because capital expenditures were required, and she did not think he would think it prudent to borrow the money. One night we were at dinner with them and she sat down and announced to him (and us) that she had gone to an auction that afternoon and bought a dental chair and dental equipment and that she had also leased space from an existing dentist to begin her practice.

Her husband, normally a very mild mannered man, went ballistic. She told him that she could not return the equipment or the chair and the lease was a contract. We witnessed a two hour tangle. At the end of it she apologized, he gave up, and she has a very successful dental practice now.

Another friend, Susan, and three other women planned to meet in a hotel parking lot, leave their cars there, climb into one car and drive two hours together to make a client presentation. It turned out when they got there that the hotel had changed its policy. You could only use the parking lot if you were a hotel guest, attending a function or eating in their restaurant (all of which validated the parking).

Three of the women drove in, saw the sign took the parking ticket and decided to park there and pay the full parking rate, even though they were not a guest, attending a function or eating in the restaurant.

The fourth woman drove in and spoke to the attendant. She explained that she was not a guest, attending a function or eating in the restaurant but that she wanted to pay full freight. He told her that was against the rules, and she had to leave. He would not back off his position. She ran and told all the others as she exited the parking lot. The other three piled into the joint car and followed her twenty minutes out of everyone's way to the next exit so she could leave her car there.

BALANCE THE TENSION BETWEEN FORGIVENESS AND PERMISSION

One of the most successful life insurance professionals I have ever met never asks for permission. Once you introduce him to someone, he believes that the contact is his. He will email and call that client/ prospect without talking to you about it first. Some referral sources are offended by this behavior. His defense is that if he asked first they may very well say no, and if that was true, nothing would ever happen. There would be no sale and the person and his/her family would not have adequate coverage. So he forges on.

I spoke to a businessman recently who is very slow and methodical in his thinking. He has a junior partner who is quick and a risk taker. The junior partner knows that when he asks permission, it can take forever to get an answer, so he now forges ahead and does what he wants to and tells his partner after he had done it.

I asked the older partner how he felt about this. He said he could not really say he approved of it, but he understood it and, because he does believe the junior partner is competent, ethical and good intentioned, he is okay with it.

CRACK THE $$ CODE
STRATEGIES TO DECIPHER THE CODE

Risk taking is an essential part of getting ahead.

Understand and evaluate your risks before you take them.

Invest in yourself.

Sometimes it is better to ask forgiveness than permission.

CODE No. 7 | Persistence Wins the Race

WHEN I WAS YOUNG MY FATHER, ONE OF THE MOST IMPORTANT AND favorite people in my life, consistently told me, "You will never be the prettiest, you will never be the smartest, you will never be the most anything. The only way you are going to get there is by staying on the path, never giving up and constantly striving to be the best that you can be.

"You will find, as life goes on, that one by one those who started off prettier than you or smarter than you will fall off course, and you will end up at the head of the parade. You will end up at the head of the parade only because you never gave up. You persisted, and that is all that matters."

That of course is not the whole story but rather the first of three lessons that, when woven together, sent a very strong message. The second lesson happened when I was admitted to Smith College and my father figured out that I did not want to go because the girl on the cover of the catalogue was beautiful and I knew I wasn't. I still have no idea how he figured it out but I remember him telling me very firmly – "Of course the girl on the cover of the catalogue is beautiful. Why would you expect anything else? You are pretty, and you are pretty enough. That is not a reason to consider not going."

Although that seems like a pretty shallow conversation now, believe me at the time it was daunting. The third lesson which wove the first two together is one of perspective. Having perspective and gaining perspective is also one of his constant themes. My college essay centered on the ocean. An oyster on the ocean floor has a totally different perspective from the eagle soaring above the ocean - both are viewing the same ocean from different and legitimate perspectives. It is the combination of persistence and perspective that leads to unbeatable conclusions.

One of my father's learning lessons to me was to memorize, recite and understand "Columbus" by Joaquin Miller.

Columbus
BY JOAQUIN MILLER

BEHIND him lay the gray Azores,
Behind the Gates of Hercules;
Before him not the ghost of shores,
Before him only shoreless seas.
The good mate said: "Now must we pray,   5
For lo! the very stars are gone.
Brave Admiral, speak, what shall I say?"
"Why, say, 'Sail on! sail on! and on!'"

"My men grow mutinous day by day;
My men grow ghastly wan and weak."   10
The stout mate thought of home; a spray
Of salt wave washed his swarthy cheek.
"What shall I say, brave Admiral, say,
If we sight naught but seas at dawn?"
"Why, you shall say at break of day,   15
'Sail on! sail on! sail on! and on!'"

They sailed and sailed, as winds might blow,
Until at last the blanched mate said:
"Why, now not even God would know
Should I and all my men fall dead.   20
These very winds forget their way,
For God from these dread seas is gone.
Now speak, brave Admiral, speak and say"—
He said: "Sail on! sail on! and on!"

They sailed. They sailed. Then spake the mate: 25
"This mad sea shows his teeth to-night.
He curls his lip, he lies in wait,
With lifted teeth, as if to bite!
Brave Admiral, say but one good word:
What shall we do when hope is gone?"   30
The words leapt like a leaping sword:
"Sail on! sail on! sail on! and on!"

Then, pale and worn, he kept his deck,
And peered through darkness. Ah, that night
Of all dark nights! And then a speck—   35
A light! A light! A light! A light!
It grew, a starlit flag unfurled!
It grew to be Time's burst of dawn.
He gained a world; he gave that world
Its grandest lesson: "On! sail on!"   40

My father's lessons are some of the most important I have ever learned, and I am grateful for them.

SETBACKS HAPPEN

Persistence is more than staying on the path; it is getting back on the path when you are knocked off it. Life gives us two types of breaks – bad breaks and good breaks. The goal is to minimize the bad breaks and to maximize the good breaks. It is foolish to think that we will not receive as many good breaks as bad breaks. All of us will. That is a universal truth. Many times in my professional life I have had to deal with setbacks. There are no short cuts. You just have to push through them. Along the way you can develop practical skills to minimize them.

A colleague, Carrie, told me about an upset that occurred early in her career. In her late 20s she was a partner in a boutique architectural firm. The firm was relatively new and the founding partner (who was 25 years older than she) started it because a significant client had hired him to design a major building. She worked side by side with him for two years. They hired junior staff. He

"Actually I'm an overnight success. But it took twenty years" — MONTY HALL

made a decision to hire three more professionals, and she agreed (without a full understanding of the economic consequences of that action. Even though she was a partner she owned a very small stake in the company and did not feel that it was okay to ask those questions). Pretty soon the finances went upside down and the founder went to her with a proposal to change her compensation structure from salary/bonus to a very reduced salary plus commission.

She was flabbergasted and had no idea why he would be doing that. He told her it was because "she was a rainmaker" and this would give her an incentive to propel her career forward. He showed her projections that if she brought in "x" amount of new business she would receive "y" amount of annual compensation. She tried to talk to him, but he did not budge. She did not think she had any alternative but to leave the firm, agonized hard about it and made a decision that she was never going to work for anyone else again or have anyone else as her partner. She was going on her own, and she told him so.

He was flabbergasted – that was not something he ever thought she would do. She left him and the firm. When she told me this story it was fifteen years in her past and she said that only in retrospect did she figure out that he must have been having extreme financial trouble and thought that because she was a "star", reducing her salary (and therefore the firm's expenses) and offering her the incentive of commissions would work.

Her inability to ask the financial questions, his inability to put them on the table and her knee jerk reaction that there was no option but to leave lead to a perfect storm. She has no regrets about the path she took but also wonders what would have happened if open, honest discussions had occurred, advisors had been brought in and other solutions considered.

TRUST YOUR GUT

If the situation does not seem right at the beginning, or the client does not seem like a good fit at the beginning, act accordingly. In my entire career that has never changed. When it starts off wrong it ends up wrong. Dreaming and hoping that it will turn around is foolish. If something does not seem right at the beginning. just don't get involved.

The corollary to that lesson is, if you have ignored your gut and are now in a situation that is sinking, get out of it. When everyone at home knows because you crossed the threshold in a foul mood and took it out on them, when your secretary is afraid to put the call through because she knows who it is on the phone, get out of it.

As a lawyer I have learned to say: "For whatever reason this is just not working. You have paid me this, and I am giving it all back to you – a 100% refund. Find another lawyer. We are done." (And I follow that up with a letter).

BE FLEXIBLE

While persisting, it is also important to be flexible. Keep you eye on your goal and don't be knocked off when life takes a different turn. Learn how to pivot.

I am a trust and estates attorney, and that was not at all what I started off to do. After I graduated from law school, I went an additional year and received a Masters in Taxation degree. I was hired by a 50 person law firm as a corporate tax associate. There was only one other woman in the law firm. Two weeks before I was to begin, the managing partner of the firm called to tell me that the head of the corporate department had left the firm and taken all of the corporate clients with him. He told me that they still wanted me, but they did not know what I would be doing as there was no corporate work left. Shortly before I started working at the firm, the litigation department took the personal injury case of woman who had been killed by a car.

The client was the woman's daughter - a hustler from the Combat Zone of Boston. (And for those of you who don't know what that means, the difference between a hustler and hooker is that a hustler is someone who "hustles" a man out of money by charging him $30.00 for a $5.00 bottle of champagne, keeps him intoxicated and keeps the "hustle" going). The hustler kept hitting on the male litigator on the case, and he was becoming increasingly uncomfortable in dealing with her. When he found out that I - a young female associate - was starting with the firm, and they did not know what to do with me, he went to the managing partner and asked him to assign me to the case to handle the probate administration of the mother's estate and work with him on the client matter so that he would never have to be in the room alone with the hustler again.

That is how I became involved with trusts and estates – a field I am much better suited to than corporate law.

NEVER STOP LEARNING

We all know that life is a journey – not a destination. And that journey should be filled with life long learning – not just about your core competence, which is an obvious ongoing, need but about skills that are related. Go to experts and invest in yourself to improve yourself on a regular basis.

FOCUS ON YOUR CORE COMPETENCE

Staying abreast of current developments in your field and discussing issues with your peers is of paramount importance. Join committees. Do the work. Serve with a purpose. Not only does that improve your technical knowledge; it exposes you to your peers.

Being known in your field starts with your peers. Doctors know who good doctors are. Lawyers know who good lawyers are. Accountants know who good accountants are, and so on. When conflicts occur, when other referrals need to be made, when someone asks who would be a good co-panelist or co-author, the recommendation will be of someone they know, have witnessed and whose competence they trust. The world has become very interconnected.

Force yourself to stay on the cutting edge of knowledge. Force yourself to attend presentations and seminars that are out of your comfort zone. Reach higher. When a new law passes or a new trend in the law is on the horizon I will make sure I teach a class on that topic, present a seminar on that topic and/or write an article on that topic, because I know that will force me to pull together all of the material currently on it, think about it and understand it.

INVEST IN YOURSELF

When I began my public speaking career I gave seminars and was very confused as to why even though I thought I did a good job no one in the audience hired me. I started to think about it and realized that there was no way I could figure out on my own how to have audience participants hire me, so I found a company that specialized in speech improvement – not in diction or syntax but in communication with the audience. I paid what seemed to me to be a tremendous amount of money for my first lesson with the owner and explained my predicament.

He asked me to start my presentation. Five minutes into it he stopped me and said, "I know exactly why no one in the audience is hiring you – you are a girl. You stand up there and speak and give the audience the right information in a well organized, articulate way. You want to show them you've done your homework, to get an 'A'. The problem is, people don't hire people for that reason. They think you earned that 'A' – that you have given them very valuable information - and they will take that information home, make an appointment with their own attorney and have their own attorney solve their problem.

"If you want the audience to hire you, then you must create a relationship with the audience, and that is not about giving them content. It is about developing a rapport while you are giving them good information. That is done by telling stories, by telling jokes, by asking them to participate, by polling them at the beginning and finding out what is on their minds, by asking them to jot down questions to ask you later, by taking action and including them in your conversation.

"The other two essential points are to make sure you ask for the business – don't assume the audience will figure out what you want - and make sure that you have developed a follow up plan. Obtain their contact information so that you can send them a thank you, an e-mail, a letter, an offer for a complimentary appointment, a phone call."

I have never forgotten those lessons and I am not sure that I would have figured that out without paying for that advice.

BECOME WEB SAVVY

It is very difficult to survive in the business world today without the web and what it offers. The web can be a revenue base for e-commerce or online transactions. It can be a "calling card" that prospective clients surf to find out if you are qualified and if you appear to be compatible. It can be a way to network and to partner.

How you present yourself on the web is very important, as is spending money on a web designer and thinking through the content and how it is portrayed. How you use the web, in part, depends on your professional life. If you are part of a larger organization, then it is likely that the marketing department will put forth your image and your marketing presence. It may include a page that pertains to your biography. If so, make it your responsibility to provide your updated information and follow through to make sure it becomes visible.

If you have your own business, you will probably have your own website. Make sure it is updated regularly, and every few years, as technology improves, look for ways to improve the site. Compare your site to those of your peers and competitors. Are there features you should add? Is there a way to bring information forward you have not thought of?

If you are just starting or don't need a full website, then check into www. whispertreet.biz. That site, and others similar to it, allow you, for a very modest fee, to have your own website. It is easy to create and easy to update.

Along those lines it is a good idea every few years to spend the time and the money to get a high quality stock photo of yourself that can be emailed when requested. And from my experience that is not easy to achieve. It is easy if you are young and beautiful. As you age, spending the time and the money to have your hair and makeup professionally done in advance of a shoot with a professional photographer is key (and not cheap). Also, speaking for myself (as someone who seems to blink constantly in front of camera lights), it can take 30-40 photos to get one that is worth using. In these days of digital photos that is easier to do than ever before.

Sign up for a search engine, such as www.googlealert.com which is not part of Google. You select a certain number of search terms (your name, a professional specialty that you are interested in, your competitors' names, your mentors' names) and for a modest amount of money it combs the web and reports to you weekly by listing all the places that the search terms are mentioned on the web and linking you to the source. Until I subscribed to this service I had no idea my name appeared on many places I did not even know existed .

Remember that the cyber world is transparent and can last forever. The way that you project yourself on the web, the connections you make through connection websites such as LinkedIn, Facebook and Twitter may very well be viewed by many, many people. The choices you make now on how you present yourself and what information you choose to reveal will be difficult to revise once released into cyberspace. Be responsible about any content you put forward. Be professional and get approval before reporting on anything that happens in your workplace.

IMPROVE YOUR TIME MANAGEMENT SKILLS

The most important asset you have (besides your health and your brain) is your time. You should give considerable thought to how you spend it – both

"You may have to fight a battle more than once to win it." — MARGARET THATCHER

long term and short term. If you are not accomplishing what you want to or if you are putting off things you should do("I don't have time to exercise" or "I just don't know where the day goes" or "Everything I thought I was going to accomplish today did not happen") then you need to understand time management.

That means focusing on what you do want to accomplish and mapping it out so it happens. Do the hardest tasks first. Get them out of the way. Make that call that you don't want to make. Write that letter you did not want to write. Clearing that stress will make the rest of the day easier.

Do your mundane tasks once. When sifting through the mail (snail mail or email) immediately sort and throw out what is not relevant.

Put similar items together. Put all bills together, for example, so that when you sit down to pay them, you are not sorting through the pile again to find them.

Set aside time for the fun stuff too – exercise, dining out, going to a museum. Scheduling events makes it more likely that the people you wish to invite will be available.

There are time management classes and there are time management tools you might purchase to help you organize your time and free up your life.

WORK THE OTHER SIDE OF YOUR BRAIN: GET CREATIVE

When you take the time to be creative and look at the world differently you will look at what you are doing differently too – different colors will appear. More details will jump out. Different connections will happen. Take a photography, art, sculpting or dance class. Take a cooking class. Travel. Work in a different environment. Change your routine.

Two years ago sitting outside in Venice, drinking cappuccino, I opened *Personal Best: Step by Step Coaching for the Rest of Your Life* by David Rock, a book a friend had recommended. The book asked me to select an area of my life I wanted to improve. I picked "Creativity" and did the exercises, answering the questions he posed. I am an over thinker type who is always skeptical, yet open to new ideas and being in Venice I decided to give it a whirl.

I had been struggling with a legal/ethical concept I had seen happening in many families I advised. It dealt with the issue of how you go about determining the competence of an elderly parent. I had been toying with the idea of writing a conventional article for a legal journal on the subject. By the time I was done with David Rock's creativity exercises, my mind had leaped to writing a screenplay based on a real life story I had been involved with.

I wrote the screenplay. It may or may not ever be a movie or TV show - who knows? What I do know is that by spending about four hours answering questions that provoked creativity I ended up doing something fun that had never occurred to me before and that I am sure is the first step on a journey to writing outside of the traditional legal, world yet still conveying messages that are important to me.

LEARN HOW TO JUGGLE

Susan Bart, a successful lawyer in Chicago told me that she had tried unsuccessfully to learn to juggle for years. Finally one day a former Russian circus performer taught her to juggle in fifteen minutes. She learned that you watch as your hand releases the ball into the air but you can't watch your other hand catch the ball because you need to watch the next ball you are tossing. (If you see your toss, your brain will know where to catch the ball without even watching it.)

That helped her understand that it is imperative to have good practices and systems for filing client and reference materials and procedures for handling certain types of repetitive action. That way, when she releases the ball, (whether it is to delegate to her secretary or associate or while waiting for the next step to be taken by the client or someone else) she can trust her procedures and systems will catch the ball when it comes down and remind her when she needs to take the next step. In the meantime she does not have to keep watching the ball.

CRACK THE $$ CODE
STRATEGIES TO DECIPHER THE CODE

Ride through the turbulence; stay the course.

Setbacks happen. Deal with them.

Maximize your good breaks and minimize your bad breaks.

Trust your gut.

Never stop learning.

Stay competitive.

Conclusion

CRACKING THE $$ CODE IS EASY ONCE YOU GIVE YOURSELF PERMISSION TO succeed and understand that it is your (and only your responsiblity) to acheive your goals. You must understand your own worth, value your contributions, stand up for yourself and never give up.

Recommended Resources

BOOKS:

Overcoming Underearning: A Five Step Plan to a Richer Life, Barbara Stanny, Collins Business Books 2007

Secrets of Six-Figure Earning Women: Surprising Strategies to Up Your Earnings and Change Your Life, Barbara Stanny, Collins Business Books (2004)

Prince Charming Isn't Coming: How Women Get Smart About Money, Barbara Stanny, Penguin (Non-Classics): Rev. Upd edition 2007)

Toxic Work: How to Overcome Stress, Overload and Burnout and Revitalize Your Career, Barbara Bailey Reinhold, Plume (1997)

Free to Succeed: Designing the Life Your Want in the New Free Agent Economy, Barbara Bailey Reinhold, Plume (2001)

Mentored by A Millionaire: Master Strategies of Super Achievers, Steven K. Scott, Wiley 2004

Personal Best: Step by Step Coaching for the Rest of Your Life, David Rock, Simon & Schuster Australia (2003)

Toward a new psychology of women, J.B. Miller, Beacon Press Boston (1976)

The Healing Connection: How Women Form Relationships In Therapy and In Life, Jean Baker Miller, M.D. and Irene Pierce Stiver, Ph.D., The Jean Baker Miller Training Institute, Stone Center, Wellesley Centers for Women, Wellesley College, Wellesley MA www.wellesley.edu

WEBSITES:

www.googlealert.com
www.whisperstreet.biz

IMAGE CONSULTANTS:

Ginger Burr
Total Image Consultants
WEBSITE: www.totalimageconsultants.com
EMAIL: ginger@totalimageconsultants.com

Susan Cervini, Fashion Consultant
The Closet Consultant
139 Budlong Street
Hillsdale, Michigan 49242
TELEPHONE: 517-439-5840

Cynthia C. Gardner
EMAIL: cynthiacgardner@comcast.net
TELEPHONE: 508-454-6664

Diana Moore
EMAIL: dmoore0511@comcast.net
TELEPHONE: 978-371-0188

STRATEGIC CONSULTANTS/COACHES:

Cindy Adams Harrison, Ed.D, LICSW
WEBSITE: www.tdavidow.com
EMAIL: drcadamsharrison@gmail.com

Thomas Davidow, Ed.D
WEBSITE: www.tdavidow.com
EMAIL: tom@tdavidow.com

Karen Kahn, Ed.D
KMAdvisors, L.L.C.
WEBSITE: KMAdisors.com
EMAIL: Karen@KMAdvisors.com

Barbara Reinhold, Ed.D.
WEBSITE: www.barbara-reinhold.com
EMAIL: mail@barbara-reinhold.com

Acknowledgements

John Annino
Judy Barber
Susan Bart
Jerri Blaney
Elaine Bucci
Robert E. Carr
Linda Cashdan
Victoria Cerulle
Susan Cervini
Donna Cohen
Celia Currin
Thomas Davidow
Cam Kelly
Kathleen Connolly
Susie Friedman
Elizabeth Guydan
Cynthia Adams Harrison
Bonnie Brown Hartley
David Howell

Patricia Jackson
Cam Kelly
Joan Kolligian
Sandra Manzella
Lauren Macaulay
Susan Miller
Brigitte Muehlmann
Deirdre Prescott
Peg Palmer
Barbara Reinhold
Mary Karen Rogers
Eleanor Mulvaney Seamans
Anne Spaulding
Dale Sinesi
Abby Slater
Lori Sutherland
Dune Thorne
Rhoda Weinman

"There is no point at which you can say, 'Well I'm successful now. I might as well take a nap.'" — CARRIE FISHER

Made in the USA
Charleston, SC
27 February 2010